Nashua Public Library

Enjoy this book!

Please remember to return it on time
so that others may enjoy it too.

Manage your library account and
discover all we offer by visiting us
online at www.nashualibrary.org

Love your library? Tell a friend!

J

YOU HAVE A PET WHAT?!

MINIATURE DONKEY

Karen Latchana Kenney

Rourke
Educational Media

rourkeeducationalmedia.com

Scan for Related Titles
and Teacher Resources

Before Reading:

Building Academic Vocabulary and Background Knowledge

Before reading a book, it is important to tap into what your child or students already know about the topic. This will help them develop their vocabulary, increase their reading comprehension, and make connections across the curriculum.

1. *Look at the cover of the book. What will this book be about?*
2. *What do you already know about the topic?*
3. *Let's study the Table of Contents. What will you learn about in the book's chapters?*
4. *What would you like to learn about this topic? Do you think you might learn about it from this book? Why or why not?*
5. *Use a reading journal to write about your knowledge of this topic. Record what you already know about the topic and what you hope to learn about the topic.*
6. *Read the book.*
7. *In your reading journal, record what you learned about the topic and your response to the book.*
8. *After reading the book complete the activities below.*

Content Area Vocabulary
Read the list. What do these words mean?

bacteria

breeders

domesticated

equine

graze

herd

livestock

mammal

predators

toxic

vaccinations

veterinarian

After Reading:

Comprehension and Extension Activity

After reading the book, work on the following questions with your child or students in order to check their level of reading comprehension and content mastery.

1. *What kind of shelter should miniature donkeys have? (Summarize)*
2. *Why do you think some people think miniature donkeys are stubborn? (Infer)*
3. *Why do miniature donkeys need to be with other animals? (Asking questions)*
4. *Do you think a miniature donkey would be a good pet for your family? Why? (Text to self connection)*
5. *Why do you think miniature donkeys are used for therapy? (Asking questions)*

Extension Activity

A zebra is another equine animal. Research zebras using the Internet or library books. Then make a chart to compare a zebra with a donkey. How are zebras and donkeys the same? How are they different?

Table of Contents

Doing the Donkey Roll

In the pasture, a young miniature donkey romps in the grass. It runs circles around the field in a fast frenzy. Its tail wags back and forth. Its ears stick straight up. Then it jumps up, kicking its back legs out. It lets out a loud, squeaky *heeee-haaaaaw*!

Now it's time to roll. It drops down to the ground and lays on a dusty patch. With four legs in the air, the little donkey rolls from side to side and grunts. That feels good!

Fun Fact
Donkeys stomp and paw at grass to make a roll patch, a dusty patch of land. They cover themselves in dust and dirt. It keeps flies away and protects their skin.

Miniature Donkey Origins

Miniature donkeys came from the Mediterranean region. They lived in Northern Africa in ancient times. Later they lived on the islands of Sicily and Sardinia, off the coast of Italy.

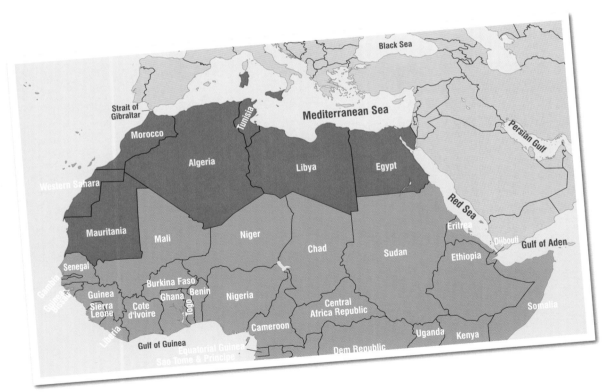

Miniature donkey origins

People used these **domesticated** animals for work. They turned grinding stones to grind grain. They pulled carts and hauled water. People used their milk too.

The Mediterranean region surrounds the Mediterranean Sea. The donkey's wild relative is the African Wild Ass from northern Africa. The donkey was tamed close to 6,000 years ago. Few miniature donkeys live in the Mediterranean now. They first came to the United States in 1929.

▼ In the early 1900s, miniature donkeys were used to carry heavy loads. Today, they are enjoyed more as pets.

Miniature Donkeys: Head to Toe

The miniature donkey is a member of the **equine** family, along with horses and mules. Like horses, a miniature donkey is a **herd** animal. This small **mammal** only reaches 36 to 38 inches (91 to 97 centimeters) tall. It has many other interesting features.

Short Mane: Its short mane sticks up.

Withers: Height is measured at the withers, a ridge between a donkey's shoulder blades.

Nose: A sharp sense of smell helps them identify food, objects, and other donkeys.

Hooves: Hard hooves are U-shaped underneath.

Tail: One-third of its tail is its swish, which has long hair.

Eyes: Donkeys can see in binocular vision, like people. Two eyes focus on one point. But they can also move each eye separately to see at the sides.

Large Ears: Ten different muscles let donkeys move their ears in almost any direction.

large ears

short mane

withers

eyes

tail

nose

hooves

9

Real Charmers

Meet a miniature donkey and you'll be charmed. They are affectionate, gentle animals. They get along well with children and adults. And they look for love and attention from their owners. They're also very smart and careful animals.

The intelligence of the miniature donkey is superior to all other farm animals. They are thinking and reasoning creatures.

Find one that's gray, black, brown, sorrel, white, or spotted. These beautiful animals also have stripes on their back and shoulders. They make a cross shape.

Fun Fact

Miniature donkeys are so gentle that they are used for therapy in nursing homes, schools, and hospitals. Therapy animals help reduce stress and brighten people's days.

Are You Ready?

Miniature donkeys make adorable pets, but ask yourself a few questions before buying one. Although they're called "miniature," they're not tiny animals. Miniature donkeys are fairly big pets. They can weigh from 225 to 350 pounds (102 to 158 kilograms).

Pet Pointers

A miniature donkey will be your pet for a very long time. They live 25 to 35 years or longer.

Can you buy more than one? It's better to have two miniature donkeys. They can keep each other company.

Is there land where a donkey can **graze**? Do you have space to build a nice shelter too? Miniature donkeys are not city animals. They need space to roam.

Miniature donkeys are very good with children and love attention and cuddles.

A Few Problems

Do you have a pet dog? Your miniature donkey might not get along with it. Groups of dogs can attack or chase miniature donkeys. That might scare your new pet.

Sometimes donkeys can be startled. They could kick or bite when scared. Most just do a little hop with their hind legs. This is a warning that they might kick.

Some people think donkeys are stubborn. They might stop and refuse to move. They are very smart animals. They won't do something if they believe they will be hurt.

Pet Pointers

Have you seen a donkey curl up its lips like it's smiling? It's not, it's smelling! This is called the flehmen response. A donkey has a sense organ in its mouth. When it flehmens, a donkey draws the scent into its mouth.

Miniature donkeys have excellent memory skills. They never forget.

Buying Miniature Donkeys

You've made the decision. You want a miniature donkey as your next pet! So how do you buy one? First check that the laws where you live allow pet donkeys. Donkeys are considered **livestock**, like cows or sheep. Some areas require livestock owners to have a few acres of land for their animals.

You can buy miniature donkeys from **breeders**. They can give you a history of a donkey's health and tell you about its parents. Or you could try a rescue farm. You'll find miniature donkeys that need new homes.

Pet Pointers

Your miniature donkey should be at least four to six months old before you take it home.

▼ *Baby donkeys are called foals until they are weaned. After that they are called weanlings.*

Your Pet Donkey

Before you bring your pet home, set up a shelter to protect your donkey from snow, rain, sun, and flies. Plan for at least 8 x 8 feet (2.4 x 2.4 meters) for each animal. Add a bedding of straw or sawdust. It should go up 4 to 6 inches (10 to 15 centimeters) from the floor. Always remove soiled bedding. Completely change it a few times a year.

Miniature donkeys also need pasture to exercise and graze. Provide about one-half to one acre of land for your pet. Put up good fencing to keep your pet in and **predators** out. It needs to be about four feet (1.2 meters) high. A woven wire fence is a good choice.

Donkeys mostly eat hay in the winter. Put hay in a hayrack. It keeps hay off the ground, clean, and free of bugs. Give your donkey mineral and salt blocks too.

During the summer, miniature donkeys graze in a pasture. Do you have any **toxic** plants? Check with your **veterinarian**. Some plants will harm your pet.

Pet Pointers

Donkeys don't need much food. They can easily get fat from grazing. Watch for a fat roll around their necks. Adjust their food to keep your pets healthy.

Fresh water is very important. Keep the water cool in the summer. Place it in the shade or add blocks of ice. Use a heater in the winter to keep water from freezing. Always keep the watering container clean.

Gentle miniature donkeys can be great fun to ride. They are strong enough to carry children. They can hold up to 75 pounds (34 kilograms).

Train your miniature donkey to pull a cart too. One donkey can pull up to two adults or children. You need the right kind of cart and harness. Donkeys don't scare easily, so they are easy to handle.

Miniature donkeys can do some tricks. Teach them how to lay down, jump, or sit on command. Some like to play with balls too.

▼ *A miniature donkey is affectionate, extremely comical and a*
▼ *joy to own.*

Take good care of your pet. Miniature donkeys should get checkups from a livestock veterinarian. They treat larger animals, such as cows or sheep.

Donkeys need yearly **vaccinations**. They also need to be treated for worms inside their bodies. Dental care is important too. Check a donkey's teeth twice a year.

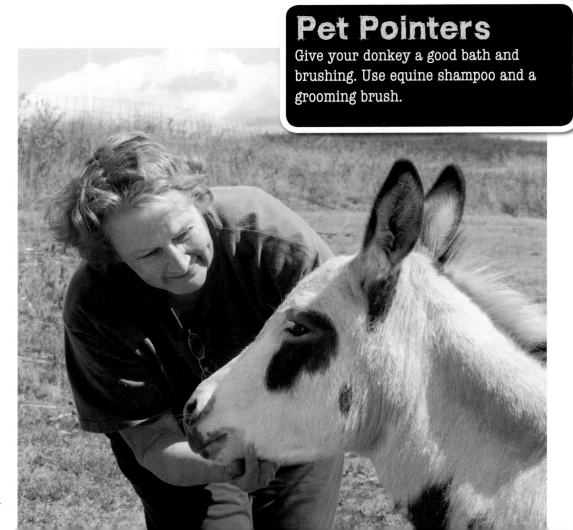

Pet Pointers

Give your donkey a good bath and brushing. Use equine shampoo and a grooming brush.

A donkey's hooves should be trimmed every two to three months. If you live in a wet area, check hooves for **bacteria**. Clean them well with a hoof pick.

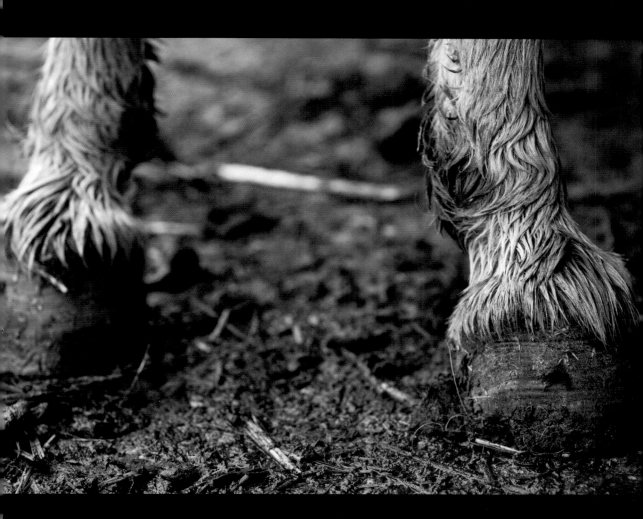

It can take a few weeks for a miniature donkey to get used to its new home. Groom it every day. Speak softly to your donkey. Spend time getting to know your pet. Soon it will settle in and feel comfortable.

You'll need to train it to wear a halter and a lead. Then you can take your donkey on walks.

Once you have a good bond, your donkey will give you lots of love. It will look for your attention too.

Miniature donkeys make great pets. They're warm, friendly, and lots of fun. Take good care of their hooves and teeth. And don't forget to give your pet hugs and rubs. Your miniature donkey will be a loving friend for life!

Things to Think About
If You Want a Miniature Donkey

- Miniature donkeys are not city animals. They need about one-half to one acre of land. They also need a shelter outside.

- Different cities and states have laws about keeping livestock. Make sure it is okay where you live.

- Own at least two miniature donkeys. Or make sure your pet has another animal it can bond with.

- Miniature donkeys have a long life span. They live 25 to 35 year or longer.

- Make sure you trim your pet's hooves and check their teeth regularly.

Glossary

bacteria (bak-TIHR-ee-uh): tiny living things that live inside animals and outside their bodies; some bacteria are harmful and some are helpful

breeders (BREED-urz): people who keep, mate, and sell animals

domesticated (duh-MESS-tuh-kate-id): tamed to live with or be used by humans

equine (eh-KWINE): of the horse family

graze (GRAYZ): to eat grass that is growing in a field

herd (HURD): a large group of animals

livestock (LIVE-stok): animals raised on a farm, such as cows

mammal (MAM-uhl): a warm-blooded animal with a spine, whose females produce milk for their young

predators (PRED-uh-turz): animals that hunt other animals for food

toxic (TOK-sic): poisonous

vaccinations (VAK-suh-nay-shunz): shots given to animals to prevent diseases

veterinarian (vet-ur-uh-NER-ee-uhn): a doctor who treats sick animals

Index

Show What You Know

1. Why do miniature donkeys roll on the ground?

2. Where do miniature donkeys originally come from?

3. Why do donkeys curl their lips?

4. How much can miniature donkeys weigh?

5. What should miniature donkeys eat?

Websites to Visit

www.animalplanet.com/pets/other-pets/8-miniature-donkey

http://detroitzoo.org/animals/zoo-animals/miniature-donkey

https://nationalzoo.si.edu/animals/miniature-donkey

About the Author

Karen Latchana Kenney is an author and editor in Minneapolis, Minnesota. She has written dozens of books for kids on many topics, from how stars and galaxies form to how to care for pet sugar gliders. Her award-winning books have received positive and starred reviews in *Booklist, School Library Connection*, and *School Library Journal*. When she's not researching and writing books, she loves biking and hiking Minnesota's state parks, traveling to new and exciting places with her husband and son, and gazing up at the night sky in northern Minnesota at her family's cabin, where the stars are vividly bright. Visit her online at http://latchanakenney.wordpress.com

Meet The Author!
www.meetREMauthors.com

© 2017 Rourke Educational Media

www.rourkeeducationalmedia.com

PHOTO CREDITS: Cover: ©Deborah Cheramie; page 1: ©lillisphotography; page 4: ©predrag1; page 5: ©Drago_Nika; page 7: ©Chronicle; page 9: ©driftlessstudio; page 10: ©Jason L. Price; page 11: ©Anne Connor; page 12: ©Scosens; page 13: ©Jack Sullican; page 14: ©marilyn schiele; page 15: ©Bildagentur Ceduldig; page 16: ©LattaPictures; page 17: ©Purestock; page 19: ©KentWeakley; page 20: ©Andrewmits; page 21: ©wyanitt; page 22: ©Daniel Dempster; page 23: ©Karine Aigner; page 24: ©Ron_Thomas; page 25: ©National Geographic Creative: page 26: ©Robert Dant; page 27: ©Dorset Med Service; page 28: ©westend61; page 29: ©oilbuff

Edited by: Keli Sipperley
Cover and interior design by: Rhea Magaro-Wallace

Library of Congress PCN Data

Miniature Donkey / Karen Latchana Kenney
(You Have a Pet What?!)
ISBN 978-1-68342-178-8 (hard cover)
ISBN 978-1-63432-244-0 (e-Book)
Library of Congress Control Number: 2016956599

Also Available as:

Printed in the United States of America,
North Mankato, Minnesota